Under
the
Wild Ginger

Under
the
Wild Ginger

A Simple Guide
to the Wisdom of Wonder

Jeffrey D. Willius

www.bunkerhillpublishing.com
by Bunker Hill Publishing Inc.
285 River Road, Piermont
New Hampshire 03779, USA

10 9 8 7 6 5 4 3 2 1

Text Copyright ©2012 by Jeffrey Willius

Library of Congress Control Number: 2012937198

ISBN 9781593731106

Designed by Joe Lops
Printed in China

Contents

Acknowledgments

In recognizing all those who've contributed to this effort and supported me during its maturation, I can only hope to be as observant and appreciative as I try to be of other things.

My dear wife, Sally, has been instrumental in the project at many levels. She's supported me with her mind and heart, understanding and making room for my commitment to the work. She's encouraged me, like the amazing teacher she is, to reexamine my assumptions. She's challenged me when she felt I might be losing my focus and then knew, uncannily, exactly when I needed her to swap her constructive criticism for unbridled praise.

My brother, Dan, has, perhaps more than he realizes, helped draw out the best of my creative core. For six and a half decades, he's been my role model, one of the men I most relate to and admire. His words and deeds of support—not to mention his own highly developed senses and ideas for subject matter—have been invaluable to me.

Then there's my good old friend, Charlie McMillan. A couple of years ago, I'd asked for his feedback on a few of the nature essays I'd been working on. His e-mail said, "Hey, these are pretty good! Someday they might be the basis for a book." That was the first time the notion of a book had ever entered my mind.

I owe a great debt to Karen Cease of Camden, Maine, for sticking her neck out to mention the title and premise of my book to her longtime friend, publisher Carole Kitchel Bellew. Until she did so, I'd entertained no pretension of seeking a publisher.

Many thanks to Carole and her husband, Ib Bellew, of Bunker Hill Publishing for responding so enthusiastically to that first glimmer of possibility, and for being able to envision its success. They've honored me with their faith, buoyed me with their encouragement, and impressed me with their skill in producing and marketing the book.

Finally, I salute editor Kate Mueller for her sensitive guidance and sharp eye, designer Joe Lops for wrapping mere words and ideas in a beautiful, tangible package that people can open and share, and cover illustrator Susan Coons for capturing the elusive beauty (or wonder) of the wild ginger.

Introduction

RECLAIMING WONDER

Do you remember how it felt when, as a child, you first discovered some little critter you'd never seen before? When, moved beyond speech, all you could manage was a breathless *wow*? That little whisper, that crystalline moment of pure wonder, is what *Under the Wild Ginger* is about.

I'm fortunate to have experienced more than my share of those joyous moments. My parents were terrific wonder role models, encouraging me to be outdoors, watching bugs, studying how water flows, digging holes—curious about everything. Through some happy coincidence of that upbringing with factors of timing, temperament, conscious decision making, and a bit of dumb luck, I've managed to keep seeing Nature—and, to some extent, life—through the eyes of a ten-year-old.

Under the Wild Ginger is a selection of my reflections, gathered over many years, on how you can experience more wonder—more of those childlike *wow!* moments— any time, every day, whether you live in the city, the country, or the wilderness, whether you're eight or eighty.

More than just suggesting things you might look for, I hope *Under the Wild Ginger* will inspire you to reclaim the childlike curiosity in your life. You don't have to go to the wilderness; you can be anywhere—even indoors. Turn off the computer and the phone; put aside schedules, worries, and expectations; be quiet and patient. Let the smallest detail capture your imagination. Use all your senses to explore it. And, most importantly, *expect* wonder.

You can do this! Kids can do this. Best of all, you and your children or grandchildren can embark on the journey of wonder together!

For any given moment, remember there's more than one way to be in it.

In the concert of life, do you tune in to the musicians? To the conductor? Perhaps it's the music, taking you far away.

All presence asks is that, wherever experience takes you, that's where you go—fully, gladly, all the way.

Give someone the benefit of the doubt.

Next time you sense the wagging finger of your judgment, imagine a plausible, forgivable reason for the offense.

See, you've just extended the rest of your fingers and turned the wag to a wave—your gesture of understanding, patience, peace.

Give yourself the benefit of the doubt.

Who are all these people whose voices we
hear inside—controlling, judging,
berating. Who do they think they are?

Remember, those voices are not yours.
While perhaps well intentioned, they have
their own baggage. Trust your own voice.

Look under things.

There's a whole world of critters that live
under things—leaves and rocks and logs.

There they tunnel and nest, beyond reach of all
but the craftiest foe—and most curious friend.
Whichever you are, you must be quick.

Describe a flavor.

Like people, the flavors we meet are easier to
judge than engage. Give them a chance,
and you may find they have a lot to say.

Get to know the sweet and earthy sides of parsnip;
draw out the grainy richness of Gorgonzola; give
voice to the buttery pungency of calf's liver.

When you think you've seen it all,
keep watching awhile.

Sailfish swatting the bait with its sword before biting;
nighthawk's corkscrew ascent before diving;
the calm before the storm.

Wonder sometimes builds in stages, where the bridge
from the interesting to the unforgettable is patience.

See right through yourself.

Much of your body is translucent. Prove it in a dark
room with flashlight and mirror.

Shine the light through your hand. Try it just behind
your ear. Put it in your mouth and see your cheeks lit
from within. Oh my, how you glow!

Say hello or good-bye to a cloud.

Clouds morph and merge all the time, but they also
come and go, magically appearing out of—
and vanishing into—thin air.

Some scattered-cumulus day, pick a smaller,
wispy cloud, or a patch of clear blue.
Then watch and wait.

Listen to your body.

Feet complain, stomachs beg, hearts sing, heads go on and on. Some of these voices are pushy, others meek; most you politely indulge.

But don't dismiss them. Pay them as much heed as you would your children, for they too are for you, of you.

Feel the pulse of a hot summer meadow.

Late summer afternoons, the meadow is a shrill cacophony, a population of buzzing, whining, whirring beings.

Like any city, this one emits one common, unifying sound, a kind of pulsing, sizzling energy. Can you hear it, this heartbeat of life?

Be a clever, appreciative witness.

Nature's pretty shy. To better your chances
she'll come out and play:

* head for places that are hard to get to
* go when others don't
* get there early or stay late
* find a point of view others may not have
  imagined
* *expect* wonder

Once in a while, look up.

Ninety-five percent of vision's range—with all its
wonders of wisp and wing, branch and beam—
lies above eye level. Don't miss it.

At night, while level eyesight obeys the dark,
the upward glance defies it, stretching a billionfold
to behold the stars.

Find your core.

Too much of life occurs at the margins—those rough
spots where we chafe against obligation, assumption,
expectation, fear.

So how do you find your sacred center, that place
where all time is now? Go where your heart leads; it
alone knows the way.

Get polarized sunglasses.

Squint as you will; you'll never crack the hard
enamel glare that sun bakes onto water.

Polarized lenses, though, like magic x-ray glasses,
dissolve the glare, reveal the mysteries of that alien
world behind reflection.

Try a food you've never tasted before.

Food is fluent in any language. Let it be your
guide to distant lands, your introduction to other
cultures and new friends.

At home or abroad, explore new flavors, challenge
your tastes, feed your sense of adventure.

*Close your eyes and identify
mystery objects by touch.*

We depend so much on eyesight to figure out
what's what. Does this cheat your other senses?
Could you do without it if you had to?

A pencil might be easy, or maybe an egg. But can
you tell nickel from quarter, lemon from lime?

Play.

How sad to toil for a lifetime, striving for days of leisure, only to forget, along the way, how to play.

Pretend, create, build, or just be silly today. Do it with someone or just with Nature. Water, sticks, pebbles, snow—she provides the toys.

Chew your food longer.

There's this amazing little place where even the simplest of dishes is explored, savored as if it were the last meal of your life.

It's a place where eating's not rushed, never a chore. So bring all your senses and appreciate the glorious gift of food.

Find your moon shadow.

Sun shadows fall heavy on the earth—stark,
stretched, hard-edged forms, so common we barely
notice their attachment any more.

Moon, though, lays down her strokes gently, subtle
shades of black on black. Knowing her time, she
works best when facing both earth and sun.

Delve into microspace.

The universe is immense beyond comprehension. Yet
this vastness is reflected, literally at our fingertips.

Let a microscope convey you to that deep inner
space. Coax patterns and textures out of hiding; play
among minute beings to whom you are a planet.

Appreciate Nature's patterns.

Nature can seem so random. Yet her elegant
alignments, rhythms, unisons, and repetitions suggest
the hand of a deliberate intelligence.

Hear its wisdom in cricket song and echo;
see it in wood grain and feather; know it in
fingerprint and heartbeat.

When problems beset you, refocus on possibilities.

In every human condition lie the seeds of its
opposite. Pain does not exist without the hope of
relief. Same with sadness, discord, and want.

Nurture those seeds; sprout and grow with them
despite the poor soil.

Hold things up to the light.

Leaf, fish scale, agate, maple seed. All have inner beauty—veins, cells, grains, layers, colors—revealed only in their translucence.

Let the sun or your own illumination be your x-ray, curiosity your power—and see deeply.

Find color in a white-gray winter's day.

Summer's colors are a feast; winter's, a tasting.

Savory shades of tenacious-oak-leaf brown. Sharp notes of dogwood-stem burgundy and chartreuse. These and a thousand other hues brave the cold, tempt the discerning palate.

Adopt a fresh perspective.

Put something you've seen a hundred times on a
virtual lazy Susan. Spin it and look at it from all
sides. What new aspects do you see?

Once you can do this with things, maybe you can put
a new spin on matters of more consequence:
feelings, beliefs, attitudes.

See generously.

Though sensing may seem a kind of acquisition, the
words suggest it is as much about giving as taking.

Let go of agendas and schedules; *surrender* the
cell phone; *commit* your time and presence;
pay attention and *share* wonder.

Find ghost stations on an old radio.

Some clear night, turn on an old analog radio (the kind with a tuning knob). Find the faintest signal you can detect between the major stations.

See if you can catch a station break to learn how far those lonely waves rolled through dark, starry skies to find you.

Garden.

We come from the earth, and there we return. Gardening celebrates this elemental connection in a most wondrous, reciprocal way.

Growth, flowering, fruiting—it's all shared, not least the nourishment. The potential, you see, lies in the gardener as much as the seed.

Introduce yourself to your spirit.

You are more than you think, more than you feel.
Others see it every day, that aura that walks
with you into a room.

Be aware of your spirit; converse with it;
make sure it's someone you want to be seen with.

Blow toward a candle from across the room.

Air's like this magical, invisible liquid. It ebbs and
flows, pours in to fill voids, and lifts huge things—
like roofs and airplane wings.

Like a wave, your breath rolls across the void.
Will there be enough left of it to make lap
that tongue of flame?

Close your eyes at night
and describe the colors you see.

Pulled shades shut you in a small, dark room—one
sealed, you might expect, in sheer, flat blackness.

Surprisingly, dilute colors seep in through synapse
cracks and pool in mind's eye, lighting your way . . .
at least to sweet dreams.

Bless a stranger with your thoughts and deeds.

You know how it feels. A stranger smiles and offers
a kind word, perhaps sees your need and helps.

Be that kind presence today; wish passersby well.
Know they might walk in darkness today,
but for the light of your being.

Value learning more than knowing.

Certainty's such an ill-fitting garment.
Perhaps it suited you once, but you and
your truths have changed.

Asking, learning, and simply being are all cut
of the same miracle cloth; they fit you and the
present moment perfectly and always.

Study dust.

Turn on a lamp or flashlight in a dark room.
Sit still and watch the tiny airborne
particles floating around.

What sizes and shapes do you see?
Where do they come from? How long till
gravity has its way with them once more?

Play a wine glass.

Crystal becomes string, finger becomes bow,
in this showy acoustic amusement, this lesson
on the flexibility of everything.

Hold the stem with one hand. Dip a clean finger in
water and rub 'round the rim. Experiment with
speed and pressure. Be patient.

Experience life with all your senses.

Might the storied sixth sense be simply the instinct
to fully employ the other five?

When one sense draws you to something, enlist the
others, too. Let them play with one another: smell
colors, feel tastes, see smells.

Talk back to Nature.

Just as we listen to Nature, Nature listens to us.

She hears that little gasp at a wonder beyond words;
a cry of conquest o'er peak or whitewater; our
answering a gullible bird; even our unspoken thanks
for the privilege of the conversation.

Look in the water at night.

In river, lake, or sea, as on land, some creatures come
out only after dark. Catfish prowl, crayfish scavenge,
leeches lace the shallows.

For a few curious moments, your flashlight is an
unwelcome sun. Look and learn, but be quick and
spare those night-accustomed eyes.

Cook.

You are what you eat. Make sure both are works
of art. Let Nature's bounty be your medium; your
nurturing creativity, your method.

The color, the texture, the flavor—not to mention
the *love*. Is there another art form that appeals
so to *all* the senses?

Play wild game tracker.

Look for tracks in soil or snow; note their
stark account of a passing moment in some
wild critter's life.

Who was it? Where was she headed? Was anyone
following? Did he make it? Read the story and be
grateful you're the tracker.

Listen underwater.

Slip into an alien world, one of slimy, legless
phantoms, where sound carries forever through an
atmosphere devoid of air.

Next time you swim, listen for the unearthly noises:
muffled splash, shrill whirr, cryptic click.
Can you imagine their origins?

Travel.

You needn't go far, just beyond the borders
of your assumptions.

Take the backstreets; make the gifts of people,
place, and perspective your souvenirs;
and go home forever changed.

Smell a ladybug.

Elegant ladybug, so demure her disposition,
so reluctant her showy flight. But there's
a limit to her decorum.

Annoy her and those legs secrete a foul smell. A
hard-shelled harlequin hemisphere with attitude.

Turn over plant leaves.

The two sides of a leaf are as distinct as our own
fronts and backs—different in color, texture,
structure, function.

And leaves hide lots of critters, their refuge from
snapping beaks, merciless sun, and mammoth
raindrops. Look, but respect their sanctuary.

Capture a single snowflake.

How fragile, how fleeting this crystalline moment.
Take it in, for this fickle vision may melt or
evaporate before your very eyes.

Let each inimitable flake remind you of your own
impermanence, your own stunning uniqueness.

Crush a familiar leaf or bud and smell it.

As beautiful as a plant may look,
some are like chocolates: you have to get
inside to reach the good stuff.

Pine needles, geranium, sage, juniper berry,
creeping Charlie—just a few that may surprise
and delight you with their fragrant essence.

Get a charge out of static electricity.

Some dry winter day, shuffle slippered feet on
carpet and touch someone's unsuspecting skin—
someone who can take a joke.

Rub a balloon on your hair and watch it cling to
things. Pull off a sweater in the dark; see and hear
the miniature electrical storm.

Behold the cream in your coffee.

Is there anything so dark, yet so clear, as black
coffee? And the smell . . . you start thinking of
it in the middle of the night.

How could it get any better? Use a glass mug,
add cream, and watch dusky thunderheads
billow in a mahogany sky.

Praise yourself; say it out loud or write it down.

Who do you think you are? If this strikes you less
as a constructive reflection than an admonishment,
you might want to think again.

Channel all that energy you waste on self-doubt
and false modesty back into shining your light,
and see the wonder of who you are.

Take a gander at ghostly geese.

Those late-fall nights when you're outside,
keep your ears open for what may sound like
a crowd of people jabbering in the distance.

Look up and find the stringy V of geese slicing
south two thousand feet up, dimly lit against
the black by ambient earthlight.

Smell your dog.

It's hard to overstate how much your dog smells you.
Though you can do it but a thousandth as well,
why not return the favor?

Sniff loudly 'round his collar, behind her ears—
dogs like that. Try the feet; they might have a warm,
nutty smell, especially after naps.

*Meet all the little critters that hang
out on your garden plants.*

Your garden's a cafeteria to a menagerie of
bugs and blights—gnawers, suckers, cutters,
rotters. And that's not all.

You'll see others there to dine on the diners.

Hum in the bathroom.

Tiny spaces with hard walls make good echo chambers. (Public restroom stalls are the best.)

Hum a scale of notes till you hit one that resonates. You'll know it when you hear it; it sounds like the echo's inside your head.

Be aware of negative space.

In Nature, as in life, we can see more if we notice not just things, but the spaces between things; not just sounds, but the silences they frame.

Far from empty, these inhalations in the song of creation are what make each note so clear, so sweet.

Listen for the voice of snow.

So self-possessed in its lovely stillness, snow's not something we associate with sound. Under pressure, though, it has a lot to say.

Walk or drive on snow and heed its powdery whispers, wet slurps, compacting thumps, and dry Styrofoam squeaks.

Don't think too much.

Your thoughts are not who you are. Care for them as you would your child: observe them, hear them, but don't let them control you.

Being—your loving openness to each moment— is what makes you who you are.

Drink in a glass of beer with your eyes.

Drinking beer from the can is like putting out fresh flowers without unwrapping them first.

Pour your beer. Taste the rich amber color. Savor the creamy foam topping, the spritely strings of bubbles. Relish the Brussels lace of descending foam as it unfurls on glass.

Hunt night crawlers with a hose.

Smart hunters know how to make their quarry come to them. Savvy fisherman and students of Nature, too.

Aim a slow stream of water at a patch of lawn. Sit down, wait, and watch for slithering life flushed from dark, earthy lairs.

Unravel a smell.

Smells, like sights and sounds, interweave in the splendid tapestry of sensation that surrounds us.

Are you as curious about a smell as you are a sound? Catch the tag end of one you don't recognize and see if you can follow the thread to its origin.

Bathe in dappled sunlight.

Trees, like sunshine showerheads, sprinkle warm, liquid light on eager soil, grateful skin.

See how each gap in leaf and limb pours an image of the sun? (Eclipses, tellingly, blot these round pools to crescents.)

*Notice where others are looking
and look the other way.*

If you want to see unusual things,
see in unusual ways.

Photograph a group posing for someone else. As the
quarterback drops back, watch what the center does.
Turn away from setting sun and find rising moon.

Turn a chore into an experience.

Wash the dishes! Mow the grass! Clean the house!
How many times have you abhorred a task at the
price of its possibilities?

No matter how menial the job, strip it of expectations,
invest yourself in the sensations, and welcome it
into your beautiful life.

Try to place people by their accents.

Language is such a trip! You can follow its sounds
and rhythms to any region of the U.S.,
any corner of the world.

Listen to people. Can you separate the way they
talk from how they look? If they took you home,
where would you be?

Unload your guilt.

Should is such a loaded word, piled with someone
else's values and expectations. Don't let them put
the word in your mouth.

Find and hear your own voice. Do what you know is
right. If others won't forgive you, forgive yourself.

Wait out a chrysalis.

Nature has much to teach us about potential—
a model, perhaps, for our own inevitable
growth and renewal.

Here's a take-home assignment: Find a chrysalis.
Keep it in an airy jar till it hatches. Absorb the
lesson; release the miracle.

Celebrate your own footsteps.

A whisper through dry autumn leaves; squeals
of delight compressing dry snow; the thin chatter
of a kicked pebble.

Though they bear the weight of the world, let
your feet proclaim their joy—not just in getting
somewhere, but in the going.

Spend some time with Nature at night.

Darkness brings on Nature's nightshift. Cicada's
relieved by cricket; oriole by owl; squirrel by skunk.

Let senses better suited to dark than vision
regard the new crew as they take their turn in
the urgent business of being.

Take a trip by yourself.

If you're to have an intimate conversation,
three's a crowd.

Get to know a place, a landscape, a culture
one-on-one. Let it in, possess it, with no agenda
but your own, no need but wonder.

Study a soap bubble.

Behold the perfect gossamer globe. Its continents shimmer and oceans glow like fluid rainbows.

Let your eye search the swirling currents for your filmy reflection, a reminder of your own exquisite impermanence.

Get lost in a map.

A part of Virginia farther west than Detroit?
A European country shaped like a star?
Hawaii not our westernmost state?

Ah, the fascinating things you'll find on this anyman's odyssey aboard the ship of discovery, its sails billowed by curiosity!

Stick your arm in a compost pile.

Sometimes finding wonder is a dirty job—
but someone's got to do it! Are you curious enough
to take the challenge?

Work your hand into a healthy, working compost
heap—all the way to its core. Feel how billions of
busy microorganisms let off steam.

Fly a telescope deep into the night sky.

The stance of the naked eye stays firmly planted
here on earth. But enter the telescope's magic portal,
and gravity lets go its grip.

Set a course for the moon and stars, and soar—if not
to reach them, at least to meet them halfway.

Go fishing.

You send a message deep into a cold, dark, liquid world. You wait. Down there, as if a million miles away, an alien being replies.

With any luck, it accepts your invitation. You greet its cool, scaly beauty and thank it for coming. Mystery turns to blessing.

Track a mysterious sound.

The soundtrack of your life is a chorus of a thousand voices— whisper of air, hum of machine, laugh of water, song of living thing.

See if you can sort through the clamor and pick out just one sound. Where's it coming from? Can you figure out what's making it?

Choose the window seat and fly.

You can read a book or take a nap anywhere.
But in an airplane, you're not just anywhere;
you're at the height of wonder.

Soar between cloud mountains. Behold rivers
sewn through quilted farm fields. Bathe in
moonlight awash o'er a billowy blue sea.

Make a quiet entrance.

Nature's a wary host . . . when she knows
you're coming.

In the wild, declare special times for slow, silent
movement. Be still; walk or paddle lightly; peer
slowly 'round the next bend.

See who rides the tips of tall grasses.

Atop pointed green blades and golden seed heads,
ants scout, grasshoppers prepare for launch,
ticks sniff for traces of CO_2.

Everyone's poised for something.
Comb through summer fields and find the
opportunists—before they find you.

Hop aboard a distant trawler or freighter.

Curiosity's your pass, a romantic spirit
your conveyance, to a place just this side
of imagination's horizon.

Fancy yourself aboard, how it sounds and smells
and feels, what you'd learn, and all the salty
characters you'd meet.

Know a higher power.

Whether your divinity resides deep inside you,
everywhere, or nowhere, acknowledge the eternal
wisdom behind Nature's exquisite design.

Respect it as your mother; heed it as your best friend;
nurture and protect it as your precious child.

Bloom where you're planted.

Like a wildflower, if your roots aren't taking, extend
them deeper. Drink up your bliss when you can;
reserve some for drought.

Hold on tight, defy the elements, astound life with
your breathtaking blossoms!

Dig a hole.

History lies in layers at our feet—earth history, organic history, human history. Its secrets reveal themselves to those who care to dig.

Shales, shells, shards, all tell haunting stories sequenced neatly through time. Are you ready to listen?

Note trees' sharp contrast against a twilight sky.

That hour between sunset and darkness has its own tactile magic. Can you trace the black lace edge of nightfall?

Run your fingertips across the tracery of treetops, tatted jet black against the dwindling hearthglow of western sky.

Get into a frozen lake.

Fissures crack and groan; leaks well up and set like candle wax; bubbles, bobbers, and bluegills are frozen in time.

Keen senses prove that lake ice is no immutable whole, but a fractured raft of so many separate floes.

Turn a chore into an experience.

No matter how dirty or menial the task, invest yourself in the sensations; get in sync with the rhythms and repetitions.

Relieve the task of expectations. Gently turn obligation to intention, and welcome it into your beautiful life.

Observe observers.

You know that incredible energy that can
build between performer and audience?
Check it out from the players' point of view.

At a play, concert, or game, turn discreetly around
and enjoy the expressions of those behind you.
Applaud with *and for* them!

Don't miss the trees for the forest.

Ten thousand sardines turn as one organism.
Leaf-cutter ants pour like a river afloat with tiny,
green-sailed ships across the jungle floor.

Wonder en masse.
But pick just one individual and watch it closely.
See why life's so much closer to the edge
for the one than the whole.

Find your place in a dark, starry sky.

Planets, stars, meteors, tiny black "voids" where
a billion invisible galaxies reside—reminders,
if we fathom, of a humbling reality:

We're but minute organisms clinging to an
insignificant speck floating in endless space
for a fleeting instant of time.

*Have a tasting party: wine,
ice cream — whatever.*

Tasting, like any exploration, stretches your
creativity as well as your senses. The challenge,
you might say, is consuming.

In a blind test, you describe what you taste,
compare notes, and pick a favorite.
Then you polish off the contestants.

Touch more.

You can see, hear, smell, or taste more or
less anonymously. But when you touch something,
it touches you.

Explore this, the reciprocal sense; share it with earth,
water, and air, as well as living things. Touch . . .
and be touched.

Hear the dying gasps of bubbles.

Stand five or six feet from a sinkful of fresh soapsuds.
Blow toward the bubbles. Watch and listen.

Take a closer look: see how the bubbles connect,
how some vanish, while others merge to last a few
wondrous seconds more.

Talk with people, not at them.

What's happened to conversation? Wouldn't it be nice
if there were a little less telling, a bit more asking?

Sure, we all want to shine. But when you talk,
you're borrowing someone's attention.
Be sure to return it—with interest.

Play with a stick.

Feel it, peel it, smell it, scrape it, split it, bend it,
break it, balance it, bite it, build it, flick it, float it,
carve it, spin it, draw with it . . . *whew!*

To a kid, it's breathtaking the wealth of wonders to
be claimed in a simple stick. Be that kid.

Imagine yourself in a critter's place.

Would you worry about the past or future if you knew
you were being hunted? Could you afford not to be in
the moment if you were the hunter?

What would it take to not feel threatened by that
huge, strangely upright creature watching you?

Get into art.

Paintings and sculptures reach across centuries.
The good ones put us in touch with our feelings,
speak to us in the here and now.

But a sharp eye discovers unintentional signs—a
fingerprint, a hair, a sweat drop stain—that put you,
hauntingly, in the *artist's* moment.

Interview your alter ego.

You know that little voice inside your head?
Does it light the way for you or trip you in the dark?

Have a talk with your alter ego.
Write down the dialogue as it magically unfolds.
Engage the praise; question the scorn.

Expect miracles; be wonder.

Wonder isn't exactly something you find.
It isn't even something you look for.

Wonder is more like something you *are*. For it all
starts with intention, with a generosity of spirit, with
your abiding faith in goodness and beauty.

Explore a freshly sliced strawberry.

From its furry, white core to its tiny, golden, pear-
shaped seeds nestled in little red craters, the
strawberry is a feast for the senses.

First, devour the shapes, colors, and textures you see.
Then let touch and smell and taste have their fill.

Compare the two sides of someone's face.

We all have split personalities—at least
if you ask our faces.

Block out one side of a face, then the other. Do these
two characters look like they even know each other?

If you don't like things you see, change yourself.

What we see reflects who we are. Assumptions,
agendas, and expectations distort both,
obscure essential truths.

Remove those filters, try a new lens,
and see clearly the wonder that was there all along.

Do one thing at a time.

Trying to do two things or be in two places
at once is to fully experience neither.

Whether it's a thought, a task, a person, or a chance
at wonder, each deserves your undivided attention,
your utter presence.

Experience things as if for the first —
or the last — time.

Greet sun and fresh air today as if you'd spent a
lifetime in a cell. Like a wonderstruck child, let a
brand new world delight you.

Then turn this around. Imagine a today with no
tomorrow. Notice how your appreciation moves from
wonder to gratitude?

Welcome wonder!

There are as many ways to see as there
are things to be seen.

Open your senses, your heart, your spirit, and the
right way will automatically present itself to you.

Just the Beginning

If *Under the Wild Ginger* has spoken to you, I hope the conversation won't end here. I'd like the book to be the impetus for a new dialogue about how people from different places and life situations around the world experience wonder—and how they pass along that gift to their children.

So please share a brief account of your most memorable *wow!* moment with Nature, with other people, with life. Your entry will be given a chance at publication on my blog, *One Man's Wonder*—as well as possible inclusion in a future edition of *Under the Wild Ginger*. Just go to the "*Wow!* Moments" page at www.onemanswonder.com.